we was bois together

we was bois together

KELSEY L. SMOOT

we was bois together

Mouthfeel Press is an indie press publishing works in English and Spanish by new and established poets and writers. We publish poetry, fiction, and non-fiction. CLASH! Chapbooks Series is an imprint of Mouthfeel Press.

Cover Design by Cloud Cardona
Interior Design: Kimberly James at www.kimmiejwrites.com

Contact Information:
Mouthfeelbooks.com
Info.mouthfeelbooks@gmail.com

Print ISBN: 978-1-957840-29-1

Published in the United States, 2024
First Printing in English
$12

M◍UTHFEEL PRESS

Contents

Acknowledgements

Thank you to every reader, editor, blog, journal, magazine, and press that has ever said "yes" to my work. Poems from this collection originally appeared in the following publications:

Scalawag Magazine:
"How To Survive A G*rlhood"
"Dark Matter"
"Maxx Puts Their Arm Around Me In The Uber Ride Home"

Twyckenham Notes:
"Transitory"

Sad Girl's Club Literary Blog:
"The Body (in theory)"

Room Magazine:
(An Abridged Version of) "7 Kwansabas For Anyone Who Wants To know How To Write Poems In Place of Theory"
"Chest Binder Bliss//Top Surgery Blues"

Voicemail Poems:
"After Sula"

For Statria **(Maxx)**:

My best friend,

My sibling,

My co-conspirator,

A1, 4L, My G,

I know you finna blush when you read the poems
I wrote about you.

I'm grateful for everything you've ever taught me,
—and for the things we've yet to learn.

"How to Survive a G*rlhood"

Gay people weren't real   in my house
I was an imaginary friend   in my house
The first memory I have
Is of myself
Trying to wipe a memory away
Something torn and tender
Shrouded in fog
I wonder if I am both genders
Alien and mirage
Ambiance
And red flag
To be a girl is to constantly assess
What do I need to do right now,
To continue to be invited tomorrow?
I learned to blend into the background
Hid myself in closets   in fists   in a lost girl
Boy

Followed them like dyke Moses
Knowing damn well that
We could just be going
Further into the dark together
Into certain alienation
But sometimes it was worth seeing
Other people from my planet
One time, I was invited into the boys club

But grown men showed up
Making themselves comfortable on my couch
Rough hands
Telling me
This is not permanent
What I am
Is definitely not something I want to be
Telling me
Their goal is to fuck me

Into a sundress

But this is about much more than clothes—
You feel me?
I would say my gender is Black
My masculinity is just
How I relate to other beings
A state   An expression
A genre of human experience
When you ask me how I survived it, I say
I learned to send up a flare
I still naturally lilt my voice
Trauma bonds
And maybe some toxic ass nigga shit
But I'll be damned
If I'm going to be trapped *in your image of me*
Swallowed
On some slow, miserable death shit
If my younger self could see me now
They would ask
You chose yourself?

You're not scared to go to hell?
If my parents were still here,
Would I be looking this free?

Some girlhoods end in manhood
And we don't talk about those things
What isn't allowed under masculinity
What kept us from ourselves
And consumed with survival
I'm learning how to speak
To stand
To move in spaces
To embody the divine feminine
Honor the masculine
To see myself

One day I realized
I don't have to give a fuck
I don't have to make my parents proud
I could give myself permission
I already knew, I already felt
I know what my people look like
Whether you see us or not
And in the end
The conversation will always include me
Because Black women and queers
Will always be at the forefront of the struggle
Will always be at the forefront of the struggle
Will always be at the forefront of the struggle[1]

"Transitory"

There is danger in the middle
I ignore the warning
of querying eyes
neither fish nor fowl
excess flesh
where only muscle
should protrude from chest bone
My body
a contested site
a meeting place
for white imaginaries
Brandon Teena's squelched laughter—
ground to ivory dust
somewhere in Nebraska
a constant reminder
of what they might do to me
outside of a men's restroom
I chew my fears
into molars at night
trace them on lovers' backs
string together a personal history
from piecemeal memories
in case anyone asks
in case they write a book
in case someone wants to read

between the lines
in case I vanish

"Ships in the Night"

Broad shoulders
the pestilent bravado
appropriately embodied
only by first-born sons
I sport coolly in my gait
my thick, calloused hands
my throaty, foghorn of a voice

A daughter displaced
          replaced
by someone who could never
quite
do
          small
delicate
or otherwise *ethereal*

The ringing of shrillness
displeased
with the absence of shrillness in return
my name, shouted in foreign tongue
beckoning obedience
a clear recognition
of fastened knees
and dutiful shrinkage
My mother's rage

for all of its thunder
could not summon lightning
or make into a daughter

"The Body (in theory)"

It's taken me over twenty years
to embrace this encasement,
manifest of all things
queer:
grotesque
  deviant
    handsome

        lovely

      still
      "Crooked Sternum is seeking one
      Surgical Steel Scalpel"

      like manic monarch screeching
      "off with their heads!"
        call it
      crown shyness
      I avoid touching
      entire regions of my body
      like they aren't there
      like I'm not there

      Don't see myself in some reflections

only the kind ones
with hands and tongues
try to ignore
something vampiric
about my dysphoria—
a shameful bloodlust

Call to memory
a time before
the great betrayal
assigned fragile at birth
    freakshow
        f*g in two acts
           fair-weather d*ke

                finding something elsewhere
under the sky
    under my skin
       between my legs
       between my lungs

I'd rather be bereft of such
unimportant flesh
and all the things we call ourselves in waking hours
savoring only the taut
and tender peel
only the remnants
only the bandage
        only what is left behind

"Chest Binder Bliss // Top Surgery Blues"

I trace the indentations
where flesh and fabric
coalesce such that
I don't even recognize
My own reflection
And that feels good
My skin feels hot
and dense, a mountain of
me flattened to molehill and
I still want to be lessened

I feel along the scar line
meet for the first time
this body—forever mine
this new, foreign thing
is a dream awakened
but so damn scary
pain meds make me foggy
dysphoria shaped like
this new form, expands
although still tethered to

Backbone and sternum, marrowed and mired : *the bondage of this body*
Praise be the polyblend and good lighting, praise be the scalpel, the surgeon
The self-portraits because no one else knew how to conceal them in photos
Praise be the lovers who helped me pretend I was hollow from neck to navel
Sometimes, I still forget that they're gone, and that somehow, I'm still here
I sent a note to the anonymous recipient of my well-worn scrap of plastic
At first it said, please don't forget: a flat chest doesn't make you trans
And then I crossed that out and decided to write: this will crush you
bit by bit, a tiny suffocation every day—but it will feel like freedom

"~~boy~~ boi"

i like a boi
how this boi laughs in boi-ish ways
like me
but not like me
we touch like bois
a little rough
together, make a boihood
no context
nor precedent for how my
hands find boi
body
trembles under
boi fingers
how they knead and need
their lightning strikes
red hot how and where
i touch their boihood
their hands on my designer
boi chest
i know that they can feel
my boi heart knocking
against spare ribs
wonder if it makes me less
of a real boi
how much of my being boi
was bolstered by being

uninterrupted by another boi
how much of becoming a boi
means rejecting other bois
i take in panicked boi breaths
when i stare into boi eyes
get tripped up
start to wonder
if this is what they meant
                    by bois will be bois

"Dark Matter"

There is no wrong way to be a gay Black girl.
Butch bois and golden dyke mouths spit glitter and even
the ones who never really were jazzy or sassy or
rascally can become legitimized between the knees of straight
girls and elsewise. I don't know if I can still speak for us.
Or them. Damn these pronouns and all their dark matter.
Damn every straight girl who made me feel like I didn't matter.
I can hardly deny that I miss being a girl,
Even if I never really was one. But I know how much it means to us,
naming things and all that, binaries and all that.
Feeling right and good and even.
I've come out as so many different things, I can't keep my words straight,
back before I was jazzy or sassy or rascally or
a boy or depressed. All the gay Black girls I grew up with look happier now. Or
maybe just they're better at pretending. Matter
of fact, maybe they're just on the straight
and narrow thing because stud was once prison slang and a gay Black girl
looks like a grown man under blue lights. But I'mma even

up the score. Get our lick back. I know I can protect us.

I'm not afraid to spit glitter or spit venom or step behind us.

Pull up behind you mask or, like pre-covid or,

plastic surgeon, mask on, and cut your shit off like they did mine. Even

trans bois can be dyke matter–I mean dark matter.

Keep a strap on us like a gay Black girl.

I've never been the violent type. But I'mma always keep my niggas straight.

I look back on my life and try to keep the facts straight.

How I decided to slut out a type of joy that was never meant for us.

How I decided that I couldn't spend the rest of my life pretending to be a girl.

Even though I love gay Black girls and I'm really not either or,

just dark matter. A little jazzy and sassy and rascally and *I matter*.

I've had to learn how to quiet my rage and get on my knees and get even.

I'd like to think that I am becoming better, even

though I can't think of anything better than a Black girl, gay or straight.

So maybe not better, maybe just different, a dark matter

man, girl. A little jazzy butch queen in golden light. A little light for us.

I feel divinely lucky to live out the rest of my days as a soft boy or

whatever they will call me in 30 years. Maybe a retired gay Black girl.

I will always remember what it was like growing up gay, Black, and girl.

What it meant to us to matter, if only to each other or

Ourselves. I do not regret the girls who created my boihood. There will always be us.

"after Sula"

we gleamed that prom night like lit lightning bugs flossy something sincere our mamas gruffed up and flummoxed about wingtip shoes, and us carrying on with girls like they were boys. no small joys, despite the knowledge that we were headed to disparate camps which would teach us how to better be—we danced that night, you and me, like we had the right and nerve to insist upon one last solstice of far flung freedoms. all of us clambering for a little something sweet but feigning sour in the moonlight; something dour in the limelight. we liked to cosplay like we some eastside niggas, all puffed up and out but we still wet behind the ears so i know you finna blush when you read the poems i wrote about you. i never forgot the summer you told me you'd take me out to the country and fry me up some field snakes, or the way he never knew he wasn't blood but kinfolk just the same. how could i have foreseen the way our fireside chats would take us coast to coast, lyin' to ourselves in every city, thinking we could shake these listless, bogged down, half-baked, pre-stretched personas? i'm your biggest fan but you treat me like your biggest opp. at least i ain't no damn cop, and you left the marine corps with nothing but a few scratches. i thank god or whoever's out there for my baby boys, and the way i know how to code switch but fight the instinct every chance i get. maybe this fancy paper won't make me a real nigga but i can use it to keep us safe, you and me. i love you like how daddies supposed to love their first-born sons and i don't like to look at that too close. i love me like how mamas supposed to hate their daughters and i can't look away. i wouldn't change how it happened for anything though. i'm just saying.

"7 Kwansabas for Anyone Who Wants to Know How to Write Poems in Place of Theory"

I.

ON TODAY, I PUT DOWN THIS MANTLE
OF GOOD GRIEF—TRULY THE BEST KIND
MY HEART AT PEACE, AND MY MIND
I TRUST THAT THESE GOOD POEMS
CAN DO ALL OF THE GOOD WORK
LEFT TO ME BY THE GOOD LORDE
I AM BRAVE ENOUGH TO CLAIM IT

• FOR AUDRE

II.

EVEN IN THE HEART OF THE SUBURBS
BLACK G*RLS CAN LEARN THE GHETTO BLUES
DANCING TO ALL THE WRONG SONGS
HAIR AND HEART BROKEN OF THEIR CURVES
EVEN THEN, WE WILL FIND ONE ANOTHER
SYNC UP, LINK UP, KISS ONE ANOTHER
CALL IT KINSHIP, OR KINETIC, OR QUEER

• ON INSTINCT

III.

I CANNOT ABIDE A SLICE OF LIFE
I WANT THE WHOLE DAMN THING, TRULY
TO SINK MY TEETH, MAYBE TAKE SECONDS
I WANT THAT FOR MY SIBLINGS TOO
WANT THEM BELLY FULL AND DRUNK TOO
MAYBE THAT IS WHAT MAKES ME UNMANLY
I REVEL IN THIS RICH, TENDER DUALITY

• BOTH//AND

IV.

I CHERISH THIS ROBUST KNOWING OF MYSELF
BORN OF THE SOFT DRUM OF FINGERS
TEASING AT THE NAPE OF MY NECK
A COLD SWIG OF FRESH CITRUS JUICE
THE GNAWING OF WORDS LEFT LONG UNSAID
FEVER DREAMS AND THE WIDE AWAKE ONES
MY BLACK ASS WORLD BEYOND THE TOWER

• ELSEWHERE

V.

ON MIRRORS IS NOT A LOVE STORY
IT IS SIMPLY THE PLACE WE CONFESS
HOW BADLY OUR FOLKS FAILED TO LOVE
HOW WE RAISED OURSELF FROM A WOUND
ERASED OURSELF FROM A WOMB AND TOOK
BLOOD OATHS SINCE WE 'BOUT THAT LIFE
MAKING MIRRORS IN ONE ANOTHER FOR PROOF

• HOMEGROWN

VII.

LAUREN SHOWED ME THAT GOD IS CHANGE
THAT SKY DADDY SHIT NEVER SAT RIGHT
ON MY SPIRIT; I CAN FEEL CHANGE
SEE IT IN MY EYES, MY HANDS
THE HURT I TURNED INTO A STORY
MAYBE I DON'T HAVE TO KNOW JESUS
MAYBE MAKING LOVE ON EARTH IS HEAVEN

• SOWERS

VIII.

WHY DO YOU CALL IT A THEORY
HOW MY SKIN CAN SWALLOW THE SUN
MY CHEST, NEWLY MINTED A BOY'S
THE WAY YOU LOCK YOUR CAR DOORS
WHEN I PASS BY, DARING TO EXIST
THERE ARE MUCH BETTER WORDS FOR THIS:
MELANIN, OPULENT, YOUR PROBLEM TO DEAL WITH

• PRAXIS

"on poison"

First, we watched boys become men,
Second, we watched men become wolves,
Third, we watched wolves become fiction,
Fourth, we watched fiction become fable,
Fifth, we watched fable become gospel,
Sixth, we watched gospel become gossip,
Seventh, we watched gossip become media,
Eighth, we watched media become politic,
Ninth, we watched politic become discourse,
Tenth, we watched discourse become law,
Eleventh, we watched law become ballot,
Twelfth, we watched ballot become badge,
Thirteenth, we watched badge become body,
Fourteenth, we watched body become hand,
Fifteenth, we watched hand become fist,
Sixteenth, we watched fist become gun,
Seventeenth, we watched gun become bullet,
Eighteenth, we watched bullet become blood,
Nineteenth, we watched blood become poison,
Twentieth, we watched poison become boys

Black Trans Man Killed by Police in Florida

TONY MCDADE WAS

trans ▓ was killed ▓▓

was ▓▓

promising ▓ the day before.

The man who died ▓▓

the ▓ complex ▓ McDade ▓
was unarmed ▓ did not resist ▓▓ However,
police ▓▓ had a gun and

shot ▓▓

20

never ███████████ any warning before shooting.

██████████████████████████████████

████████████████ just ████████████████
███████████████

████ gunshots ████████████

██████████████████████████████████
████████████████████████████

██████████████████████████████████
██████████████████████████████████
██████████████████ the ██████████████
██████ life ████████████████████

██████████████████████████████ of
McDade ████████████████████████

██████████████████████████████████
was taken ████████████████ made public ██████
████████████████████████ The officer who shot
McDade is ████████ on paid administrative leave ████████
████████████████████

Still, the community is ████████████████████
████████████ gathering ████████ where he was shot with
posters reading ██████████████████ "Justice for Tony."[2]

"Black Trans Man Killed By Police in Florida Pt. II"

Tony Mcdade Was Trans
Was Killed
Was Promising The Day Before
The Man Who Died
The Complex McDade
Was Unarmed
Did Not Resist
However,
Police Had A Gun
And Shot
Never Any Warning Before Shooting
Just Gunshots
The Life Of Mcdade
Was Taken
Made Public
The Officer
Who Shot McDade
Is On Paid
Administrative Leave
Still, The Community
Is Gathering
Where He Was Shot
With Posters Reading
"Justice For Tony"

"Elegy for A *Black* Butch Boi"

we the never
dear but departed
gathered then scattered
in less than 30 dyke bars
across the country
and homegirls' houses
plus that one guy's
who tried to fuck
but moved on
when he realized
we wasn't with it

we just here for
last respects
better known as
last month's rent
and deposit
on the love nest
we rushed into

we indulgent
like soul food
maybe not the healthiest
but shit
paying two rents was
unhinged behavior

and she had that good shit
worth dying under
every night

we neither coquettish
nor fetish
served in every selfie
i was never finna smile
in that photo
i don't care that you wanted

me to pull up my pants
or wear a dress
like the other bridesmaids
bury me casket fresh
in j's on a friday

we the glue of this family
though you would never admit it
what else is keepin y'all together

like the gossip do
tryna guess if she my roommate
where our boyfriends at
if she play basketball too
with the low fade
but granny still
give her a little lemonade
when she comes around
'cause she a pretty little thing
not like that bulldagger'
granny say

that ol' manly girl
from around the way

we the lost causes
they stopped using that line
'you might like dick if you tried it'
a long time ago
slang that thang
if we pulled up with a back-pack
and that's on period
if you know you know
funny thing is–
we bisexual
but we gon die a goldstar
rather than
let a nigga talk to us like
we not that nigga forreal
we the
never got a childhood
because our mamas
didn't want us having sleepovers
with girls or boys
we the never got a pap smear

or a mammogram
because we couldn't afford the shit
and even if we could
afford the shit
we the please don't touch me
this body is my armor

we built ford-tough
we not bitch-made

we dead at the tender age
of 38
we still some babies
on our death day
we the tacit tether
we the roots
we like a coda to this hard Black life
we the original sin
we holy
reimagined at the repass
we back to being good christian girls
we just some raisins in the sun

"Maxx Puts Their Arm Around Me in the Uber Ride Home"

and somehow, we are boys again
    but this time, i allow myself to love them with my skin off
their shoulder is a marronage,
and i resile all the mannish hauntings
that had us caught up
got us fucked up
kept us locked up
and lost to one another
        we sat this close a million times before
        but still, i feel nervous to lean into them
        as we whirr over charleston streets
        under sleepy moss trees
        and i am keenly aware of their breath,
        just above my temple
maxx is 30 and drunk this night
and i realize we've spent half our lives
like lathes—cutting and turning and shaping one another
        and too, like mirrors
how they are not me,
i'm still not sure
maxx pulls me closer, until we are
blood brothers
i feel a warming joy grow in my gut
knowing we are both done
with the banal bravado of boyhood

i close my eyes and recall every tender moment between us
that wanted to be this one
i know that i will know them
for every moment henceforth
but i still grieve the ones in which
i couldn't be brave
because i was busy being a boy

      it's almost like they hear my remorse out loud—
          maxx leans in closer and says
          "you are so beautiful"
          in a voice i've never heard from them before
in an instant
we are boys
we are grown
we are grey
and we are gone
a whole lifetime passes
      i promise myself i will come up with something
      just as loving to say back to them
      someday soon
      i promise
      i will be their better, brighter reflection

but this night, i keep my eyes shut
fall gently onto maxx
into sleep
and dream about mirrors

Footnotes

1. "How to Survive A G*rlhood" is a found poem—a poem I wrote/ assembled with quotes from a series of oral histories I conducted in service of my dissertation research. Quotations were sourced from with the following interlocutors: Maxx Maxwell, Jacquilyn (Jackie) Simmons, Dr. LaTreese Denson, Tyson Marzouq, Tyler Dykes, Keena (KB) Blythe, Kabir Amari Gilyard, Bri Bolden, & Sir Lex

2. To create this Blackout poem, I used a 2020 article from Essence.com, written by Breanna Edwards as source material. The article chronicles the police murder of a Black trans man, Tony McDade, a mere two days after the widely publicized and protested police murder of George Floyd. Compared to the coverage of Floyd's much, McDades death was relatively absent from mainstream media coverage, and in initial reports, he was frequently misgendered.

Creator's Bio

Kelsey L. Smoot (they/them/he/his) is a gender theorist, a committed Southerner, a writer, and a poet. Their work and writings explore the process of identity formation at the intersection of race, gender, and sexuality. Selfhood and cultural constraints—such as masculinity and its associated expectations—coalesce in their writing. Their autoethnographic style has become a lens through which they understand their experience traversing the US sociopolitical landscape.

Having grown up bicoastal and spending most of their adult life in a state of transience, Kels draws from his eclectic life experiences both deep fear and great optimism regarding what people are capable of. This tension is reflected in his published writing, which can be found in *Barely South Review, The Guardian, HuffPost, Voicemail Poems, The Amistad,* and at their website, www. queerinsomniac.me

When not writing, Kels can be found actively engaging with their community, performing at The Space (a premiere open-mic based in Kennesaw, Georgia), perusing an antique store, or running the streets with their bois.